Broke2Rich:
The Keys to Financial Success

by
M. T. Simmons

Crystal Pointe Media, Inc., San Diego, CA

Broke2Rich: The Keys to Financial Success

M. T. Simmons

Copyright © 2014
Published 2014

Published by Crystal Pointe Media Inc.
San Diego, California

ISBN-13:978-0692330258
ISBN-10:0692330259

Cover Design by K E Designs
Photography by Still Shots Photography

Acknowledgments

God

Out of all the people in the world you hand selected me. Thank you for placing your hands upon my life. You really leave me speechless when it comes to describing my gratitude towards you. I realize the vision for Broke2Rich was so great that it would require challenges, victories, and successes you have brought me through to fulfill my calling. Thank you for always sending a word of encouragement for every excuse I tried to use from walking away from this gift. Lord you truly amaze me. You have my commitment to use this gift to make your kingdom greater. So keep doing what you are doing.

Mom and Dad

I am writing this with tears flowing, because God really gave me the best set of parents in the entire universe. Mom and Dad I really love you!!! I cannot imagine my life without your encouragement through your phone calls and text messages. Your excitement when I come home, your hospitality, honoring me, with unconditional love fill my heart with joy. My goal is to have a heart like yours to impact a nation.

Dr. Herbert Davis

Since joining Nehemiah Christian Center under your leadership, my life has changed. Thank you for recognizing the gifts in me and not withholding any words God gave to your concerning my future. You are the reason for the existence of this book. I can remember you saying at my business launch party "you've got to publish." So thank you for pushing me to finally publish.

Dr. Suki Stone

Thank you for taking on the task of helping me to fulfill my dream of publishing. I am forever in debt to you for taking me under your wing and ensuring that this book is just as phenomenal as you are.

Social Media Family

There are not enough words to express my gratitude for your support through this process. Because of you I have made the leap in writing this book. It is my prayer that this book may help your lives transition into the wealthiest season of your life.

Table of Contents

Acknowledgments..vi

Introduction: Book Evolution................................1

Prayer *"Lord Save My Finances"*.................................3

Chapter One: *The Law of Credit*................................5

Chapter Two: *The Law of Car Buying*.......................12

Chapter Three: *The Law of Grocery Shopping*.............18

Chapter Four: *The Law of Budgeting*.......................23

Chapter Five: *The Law of Dining*.............................30

Chapter Six: *The Law of Shrink my Bills*....................34

Chapter Seven: *The Law of Retail Shopping*...............39

Chapter Eight: *The Law of Swap-A-Tunity*................45

Chapter Nine: *The Law of Home Buying & Renting*.....48

Chapter Ten: *25 Commandments to Do with Saved Money*56

Chapter Eleven: *The Law of Travel*.........................59

Chapter Twelve: *The Law of Retirement*...................64

About the Author...69

Introduction: Book Evolution

Broke2Rich is a growing company inspiring everyone to think about the way they do their personal finances. Our goal is to help everyone redefine the path to financial success. Many people will find that they can continue conducting their personal and business affairs with minor changes but just in a more cost effective way. Financial empowerment can be achieved in various mediums. Currently, Broke2Rich recommends the most effective approach for financial empowerment is through social media, consultations, and the tips written in this book.

Some may wonder how Broke2Rich came into existence. The footwork of the business began in 2010 when I was sharing various financial tips through the use of Twitter and Facebook. I had no intention of making this into anything huge. In 2012, I was struggling with my careers in sales due to my lack of job satisfaction. I knew it was time for a career change.

Toward the end of 2012, my pastor, Dr. Herbert Davis prophetically encouraged me to launch Broke2Rich. Now when the word first came forth, my response was Lord thank you for confirmation because I knew there was more that I needed to do with my life. As I continued on this new journey, God kept giving me visions which prompted me to consult with my pastor. Always remember that if God shares a vision he wants to come to pass, he is faithful enough to perform it through your transition. In 2013, I officially went forth in business, with most of the initial legwork complete.

Was I prepared for what I was about to get into? No. Did I have the capital to start a business? No. Was

I experiencing personal challenges, financially? Yes. But I knew what I heard from God in launching this business and I knew I could depend on God to see me through this journey.

In this book I will be sharing many things that I have learned on my journey from Broke2Rich. The book begins with a prayer request to the Lord.

Prayer

Lord, Save My Finances

Lord I would like to say thank you for the life you have enabled me to live. And out of my heart flows gratitude for you being the head of my life. Lord, the reason I purchased/reading this book is because I need you in my life to help transform the way I handle my finances.

I may not have been the best steward of my finances in the past, but I do believe with your redemptive power I am able to change my outlook and thinking on my current financial situation. As I reflect on the healings you performed in the Bible, I am made aware that you can do the same to my financial situation. Some of my financial problems have been attributed a sense of entitlement, including emotional spending, depression, and necessity.

You are the Creator of second chances, and with this second chance I am willing to make sacrifices to see my finances turn around. God, I pray that as I continue seeking you that resources will become available through your mighty power. Lord, if a job promotion, debt cancelation, pay increase or even an unexpected check be in your will for me, then please send it my way.

As I make this transition, Lord, I must be transparent and honest with you. Sometimes I have purchased things out of greed or unnecessary need, but from this day forward I pray for the ability to say no to things that do not bring me closer to financial success.

I realize that success starts with sacrifice. Increase and challenge my giving into a/my local ministry. You have the power to make all things new and from this day forward I want to follow you forward. So, as I conclude this small prayer with you, I declare three things.

1. I see myself debt free.

2. Being broke is no longer a part of my vocabulary.

3. God I will follow your plan concerning my finances and from this day forward.

Amen

Chapter One
Law of Credit

When Christ saved us we were given a new identity, a fresh slate, and a brand new start. This same principle applies to our credit. We all began with a perfect credit score, unchanged and for the most part protected until age 18.

In life we are affected by our own decisions and the decisions of others who may have inherited the debt obligations of others. Maintaining healthy credit or improving your current credit score requires discipline. Below are some great tips for understanding and improving credit scores.

Improving Your Credit Score

1. A Credit Score is a three-digit number generated by a mathematical algorithm using information in your credit report. It is designed to predict risk, specifically the likelihood that you will become seriously delinquent on your credit obligation in the 24 months after scoring.

2. Your Credit Score is a direct correlation to how you manage your financial debt.

3. There are three credit-reporting agencies. Experian, Transunion, and Equifax.

4. A lender doesn't believe anything you have to say until they pull your credit report. So don't say anything about your credit report until they ask.

5. Credit Ratings*:
   ❖ Excellent: 720 and above
   ❖ Good: 680 to 719
   ❖ Average 620 to 679
   ❖ Poor: 580 to 619
   ❖ Bad: 500 to 579
   ❖ Miserable: Less than 500
* This information is provided by:
http://www.freescore.com/good-bad-credit-score-range.aspx

6. What makes up your credit score?
   ❖ 35% Payment History – Obtained by making your payments on time. Include types of loans: installments, revolving mortgages, student loans, etc.

❖ 30% Credit Utilization: This includes loan balance: loan availability ratio.

❖ 15% Length of Credit History: This includes the length of time you have had each individual account. The longer the relationship the better the score.

❖ 10% New Credit: Opening new credit cards could suggest you are in some type of credit crunch.

❖ 10% Credit Mix: This is a way for creditors to assess your risk to them. They are basically looking to see that one can pay back a variety of credits.

7. Your credit score determines your destiny. So choose your purchases wisely.

8. A person who manages credit well doesn't purchase what they are approved for; instead they purchase what they need.

9. Having no Credit is sometimes the same as bad credit.

10. Becoming debt free is a serious possibility. One can easily become trapped into debt because they view debt as a necessity to life

11. Have you ever wondered how your interest was calculated? Here's how: If you have a balance of $2000 with a 20% interest rate $2000 x .20 = $400 per year. $400/365=1.10 per day. $1.10 x 30 days = $33 per month in interest. Now if your minimum payment is $35 in this example only $2.00 was paid towards the

principal of the balance.

12. www.bankrate.com is an excellent resource for doing comparison shopping for credit cards.

13. Remember: a great credit score puts you in charge. A bad credit score makes you submit to your new master (the lender). Proverbs 22:7: "The rich rule over the poor. And the borrower is servant to the lender."

14. There are certain things you should never charge to a credit card. These items include bills, tax payments, eating out, or cash advances from your credit card.

15. Make it your duty to call your credit card company and ask for a lower interest rate. Keep in mind this works best if you have a great payment history. Let me assure you, this works.

16. If you want to pay off credit card debt fast then focus on the credit cards with the highest interest rates first.

17. Remember to check and see if there is an 'Annual Fee' for your credit card. It's very easy to miss because most companies will waive it your first year.

18. The Annual Fee is simply a fee charged for having a credit card in your wallet. Normally this comes with extra benefits. Example: Concierge, Travel benefits rewards programs.

19. Cash Advance Fee: This is a fee charged by a creditor, for you to take cash from a credit card as

opposed to purchasing something from a retailer.

20. Balance Transfer Fee: This fee is charged by a creditor to transfer a credit card balance to another credit card. This is generally popular when creditors are offering "no interest for 18 months" or when the interest rate is lower.

21. You are entitled to a free credit report every year. Please make sure that every year you check your credit report.

22. Make sure you review your credit report for all 3 agencies. In some cases they may not all have the same information. This is common because different creditors only use certain agencies.

23. If you are a victim of identity theft please be careful. In most cases the claim you have disputed may re-appear.

24. Use credit wisely because there will come a time when you really need it.

25. Sending in additional payments on debt can reduce the term of the debt tremendously. So make it a habit to send in an additional minimum payment of $10 above the minimum requested if you are experiencing a financial hardship.

26. If you don't have a game plan to pay something off in 1–6 months then don't charge it.

27. Place large purchases on credit cards and pay them

off immediately with your checking account. This allows you to get points/cash back for your purchases if your credit card offers this option.

28. Remember: never co-sign for friends. If you get into an argument with your friends, the biggest way for them to hurt you is to ruin your good credit.

29. If you are facing a financial hardship always make the minimum payment on all of your credit accounts.

30. If you are struggling to establish credit consider a secured credit card. A secured card requires a cash collateral deposit that becomes the credit line for that account.

31. If you are experiencing a financial hardship in which you are struggling to decide which bills to pay, pay the bills that report to your credit bureau monthly. Example: car payment, credit card, and mortgage.

32. Before repossession/loan default occurs, please contact your creditor and make arrangements.

33. Debt consolidation is not a bad thing. This is simply where you obtain one loan totaling the full amount of all of your debt. The loan amount is paid out to all of your creditors who will then be paid in full. And you only make one payment to your debt consolidation company. This helps secure a lower interest rate loan. Please be very careful with these loans because sometimes this causes people to create more debt.

34. If you tend to forget to make your monthly

payments try setting up calendar reminders.

35. Consider setting up online bill payments to avoid being late on your bills, due to mail delays.

36. Employers do use credit scores in their decision making process when hiring new employees.

37. Insurance companies use your credit scores to determine your insurance premiums.

38. If you are struggling with credit card debt, it may be a good idea to leave your credit card at home.

39. When you are serious about getting rid of debt, don't cancel credit accounts after paying the debt in full. It's better to simply discontinue using them.

40. Because interest is calculated daily for most credit cards you can save money on interest by making your payments before the due date.

Chapter Two
The Law of Car Buying

Purchasing a car isn't something done routinely. If you are unhappy with your car, payments become a burden. In this chapter we will explore tips for making a car payment that could save you money and headaches. After all, owning a car is truly a blessing.

Proverbs 10:22 states, "the blessings of the LORD makes one rich and He adds no sorrow with it."

Through this chapter you will obtain the knowledge to purchase a car with no regrets.

Buying a Car

1. Unless you are wealthy, you will probably finance a car. This is acceptable, because some debts are unavoidable and readily understood as part of life.

2. Make sure you understand all terms and fees associated with your car purchase. Example Annual Percentage Rate (APR), tags, taxes, warranty, or application fees.

3. If possible do not finance any fees, such as tags and documents, with your car purchase. Try to pay these fees out of pocket.

4. Know your credit status or credit score before sitting down to discuss financing a car.

5. Do your research from car reviews. Edmunds is a great place to do car research. Visit their website before any car purchase. www.edmunds.com

6. Making a car purchase is a major decision. It's okay to think about this overnight or for several days.

7. Being able to afford the car payment is not enough. Make sure you allot money in your budget for car maintenance and for possible insurance increases.

8. Please account for the increase in insurance in your monthly budget.

9. Young adults, be careful how you treat your parents. They will probably be the first person you run to as a

co-signer on your car loan if necessary.

10. People with below average credit scores tend to pay $2000 - $5000 more for their cars in interest alone.

11. Remember that the longer you finance the more interest you pay.

12. Make sure you shop banks for current rates. This will give you an upper hand on negotiations.

13. Know before going to the car lot what is considered a fair price for the car you are purchasing.

14. APR (Annual Percentage Rate): Represents the total amount of interest and fees associated with a loan.

15. If you have any doubt about a car purchase, don't buy. This will only lead to regrets.

16. When deciding if you want low financing vs. rebates you might want to look and compare the interest charges vs. rebate.

17. Your chances of a greater deal comes to play when you say "I can get this car for $xxxx cheaper and a better interest rate." This also lets your sales person know that you know the rules of negotiating.

18. Consider owning the car an additional two years after paying off the loan before purchasing a new car. This will allow you to save for a great down payment for your next car or build a strong savings.

19. Any time you can pay more than the minimum monthly payment on your car...do it. These monies are paid directly towards the principal.

20. It is a great practice to take a loan for the longest term and then make an effort to pay additional payments. This will do a couple of things for you.
    a. It can eliminate the need for Gap insurance. Gap insurance covers the difference between your loan value and car value., should the loan value be greater. Gap insurance is necessary if you put little money down, drive more than 15,000 miles a year, finance for more than 60 months, or have negative equity from a previous car loan.
    b. This option also gives you the reassurance that if ever you have a financial hardship then you know you can afford the required car payment.

21. Being too cheap on car repairs will come back to haunt you. For example: Purchasing tires with a 25,000-mile warranty for $200 cheaper rather than a 50,000 mile warranty is not cost effective.

22. Car warranty is everything. It would be wise to have some type of warranty on your vehicle especially while you are making car payments on your vehicle.

23. Car purchases are most often predicated upon emotions. Understanding this, don't allow a car sales person to pressure you if you are unsure of the purchase.

24. It is okay to ask other people how their car buying and maintenance experience has been for a particular

car company.

25. New Car = Higher Payment, less maintenance. Used Car= Lower Payment, higher maintenance. This will help you determine which car type to purchase.

26. Negative equity is when the loan value is more than the value of the car. When trading in your car avoid negative equity if at all possible.

27. The first offer isn't the final offer.

28. Download the application "Repair Pal" this will give you repair estimates and shop recommendations and will prepare you for maintenance on your car.

29. If you live in a city with great public transportation consider delaying your car purchase gratification by using the city's transportation, zip car, or even renting cars.

30. If you want to ensure you can afford a car, try putting the estimated car payment amount into a savings account for 6 months. Use this money as a down payment on your new car.

31. If your credit score is below average consider the following:
   a. Negotiating and accepting the higher interest rate.
   b. Negotiate a comfortable car payment and pay above the minimum amount to keep the car value and balance as close as possible.
   c. Make every payment on time for 6-12 months.

d. Research companies to refinance your car.

e. Refinance the car with the expectations of the payments being cheaper. If so, then continue making the old payment to get the car paid off quicker.

f. Go get the title after your car is paid off.

32. If you are looking for a car to buy for cash, just make sure you have a qualified and trusted mechanic to check it out.

33. Always pull the CARFAX on any used car you purchase regardless of age. This vehicle history report shows completed car maintenance, and inspections, since the car has left the production factory.

34. Before signing a lease, be aware of fees associated with going over the allotted lease mileage.

35. Be careful in leasing. If you decide to purchase the car after the lease you would potentially pay an additional finance term for purchasing the car. For Example: A 3 year lease + 5 year financing = 8 years of car payments.

Chapter Three
The Law for Grocery Shopping

Grocery shopping for most people is the most dreaded activity. For others it is the most exciting activity. Regardless of which category you fall within, grocery shopping still must be fulfilled and the challenge in America still continues.

How do you purchase more for less? Or is this even possible? I'm quickly reminded of how Jesus had a similar dilemma. In Matthew Chapter 14, Jesus was traveling town-to-town performing healings and miracles. Along the way he established such a large following. Now as the evening was approaching the disciples saw a huge problem. The disciples noticed they only had 2 fish and 5 loaves of bread to feed 5,000 hungry souls. The disciples even made the decision to send people away.

But Jesus saw a solution. He told his disciples that what they had was enough and that they did not need to send the 5,000 hungry souls away in order to feed everyone. The same goes for our budget. We must strategically shop to purchase as much food on our limited budget.

This very situation describes many of our financial situations in the grocery store. When applying these tips you should be able to see some major savings when grocery shopping.

Grocery Shopping Tips

1. Coupons are your best friend when it comes to decreasing your grocery spending.

2. Write down your grocery list from your home, not in the grocery store. This will alleviate picking up unwanted items.

3. Sign up for loyalty cards at your favorite stores and register those cards online for additional savings. Example: Walgreens has point based rewards programs that allow you to earn discounts for being a loyal customer.

4. Use the Internet to find which coupons to use for the lowest prices. Some places allow you to double your coupons.

5. www.thekrazycouponlady.com is great resource to understand where to use coupons to maximize your savings. This website also has printable coupons and offers.

6. Most of us tend to buy brand names for everything. Consider purchasing the store brand.

7. Write out meal plans and create your grocery list from this.

8. Remember the items you need may not be on sale when you need them. Because of this you should buy in bulk when you see these items on sale. Example: trash bags, toothpaste, deodorant, etc.

9. Avoid time driving across town to save 30 cents on one item. Always include your level of effort when it comes to saving money.

10. If you own a smartphone use your barcode scanner when you have an inclination that an item might be much cheaper elsewhere.

11. Avoid grocery shopping on Saturday and Sunday. This is when most families do their shopping. Therefore, the items on sale in the circular are more likely to be sold out.

12. Price matching is becoming a competitive advantage for grocery stores. Use it to your advantage.

13. Never grocery shop when you are hungry. Your risk of picking up more items is increased.

14. If you struggle making your grocery list, keep a list on your refrigerator and write down items as they begin to run low.

15. Focus on buying items that you can make and take for lunch. This is a huge money saver.

16. Pay attention at the register and verify your savings. This is very important when grocery stores are having "Double Coupons."

17. If a store is out of an item on sale, don't be afraid to request for a rain check.

18. Before you complete your grocery list, clean out

your fridge of expired items. This will eliminate one item trips to the grocery store during the week.

19. Use water as a dinner beverage instead of soda. This will decrease your caloric intake and decrease your grocery budget on beverages.

20. It is okay to buy items reduced for quick sale as long as you have an immediate use for them.

21. Make your grocery list using your smart phone grocery app.

22. With the money you are saving from these tips, be sure to set aside these funds for any outstanding debts.

23. Consider purchasing in bulk and splitting the cost with friends.

24. For more coupon opportunities, purchase or subscribe to the Sunday paper.

25. Pay attention to sales flyers at pharmacies. They tend to have better promotions on everyday use items.

26. Most retailers allow you to stack different manufacture's coupons for one item. Example. CVS pharmacy has a $1.00 off coupon and you have $1.00 coupon from Proctor & Gamble. Now you have $2.00 off one single item.

27. www.coupons.com allows you to print and link coupons to your loyalty cards with grocery stores.

28. Pay attention to retailers who accept competitor's coupons.

29. Ask your friends or co-workers to save their weekly coupons for items you might want to purchase in bulk.

Chapter Four
The Law of Budgeting

A Christian lifestyle is not about "a bunch of rules;" instead it's about setting boundaries that please God. The same concept goes for budgeting. Managing your money speaks volumes about your potential future.

Proverbs 13:16: "Every prudent man acts with knowledge, but a fool lays open his folly.

In this chapter we will explore some helpful budgeting tips.

General Budgeting Tips

1. Seek God for wisdom on how to properly align your budget to meet your needs.

2. Your budget is your financial plan for success. You don't get in your car and drive to an unknown destination without some type of GPS/directions.
– Tasha Owens

3. Analyze how much income you make per month. This will help you understand how much you have to budget.

4. In financial hardships separate your monthly mandatory bills so that you can pay them first. These are bills that must be paid monthly or certain actions can be taken against you.

5. Make budgeting easy: use smart phone applications that allow you to budget on the go. www.mint.com has an amazing application. Visit the site and set up your budget online. Then download the phone application to help manage it on the go.

6. Calculate your bills to understand what you must make on a monthly basis so you know what money is available for basic necessities then budget for entertainment or recreation This figure must include your savings as well.

7. Observe and remove those habits that are costing you the most money. Example: running one errand at a time or purchasing breakfast, lunch and dinner in the

same day.

8. Budgeting works best only if you can say 'no' and make sacrifices.

9. You must remain upfront with yourself about your current financial situation.

10. You are the creator of your budget. Do not let your friends influence you.

11. Budgeting is awesome! If done properly you will find that you can do more with less than you thought possible.

12. Make it your duty to stay under budget and not on budget.

13. Don't forget to tithe. Tithing is necessary for financial wealth and kingdom prosperity.

14. Paying yourself first with a safe monthly savings plan is a minimum of 10% of your income.

15. If you work your budget properly you might find a surprise pay raise or additional monies for savings/debts.

16. You must assign each dollar a task. In most cases budgets tend to get off task when every dollar is not accounted for.

17. Find pleasure in telling your friends you are on a budget. This will alleviate temptation.

18. If you want to be truly successful at this you will need an accountability partner.

19. Do not create your budget based upon your income guaranteeing you a certain lifestyle. Example: I make $50,000 a year. I should have a luxury apartment and a luxury car.

20. Balance is the name of the game. It's okay if you splurge once in a while in your grocery budget. Just make sure your dining budget is not over what you have budgeted too often.

21. When initially creating your budget always think worst-case scenario and work towards your best- case scenario.

22. Every three months re-adjust your budget. You may find that your spending habits change over time by simply becoming aware of what you are really spending and why.

23. If you are looking for boundaries for creating your budget, pull your last three months of bank statements. And make sure you balance your check book every month! Every year you must re-assess your financial goals.

24. "If you can't afford to tithe, save, and pay your bills, then you might be living above your means." A quote by Pastor, Dr. Herbert Davis

25. Net Worth = Assets – Liabilities: Very simple

formula and an easy way to determine your net worth. Assets are things you own. Liabilities are things you are responsible for repaying.

26. When you are struggling with upholding your budget always consider your purpose. Purpose should always override your current situation.

27. To avoid overspending, try using cash as much as possible.

28. Consider getting rid of bad habits like smoking and drinking excessively.

29. Get rid of obligations that are not your responsibility. Example: Paying a bill for a friend.

30. Your budget should include a best case and a worse-case scenario. This will eliminate stress when emergencies happen. When utilizing the worse case scenario budget, this should only be a scenario for a minimum of 1-2 months. If it goes beyond this time frame, then consider re-evaluating your budget.

Single/Dating Financial Considerations

31. Before saying "I do" you should know the current debt level of your spouse.

32. While dating, observe how your mate spends money. Is it cautiously or frivolously done? If you notice it is frivolous, you might want to observe more about how he or she currently handles his or her finances.

33. Discuss family values. Does your mate want children? Family? Vacations?

34. Pay close attention to your dining and entertainment budget. This is a category that can easily get out of hand.

35. Do not co-sign for anyone unless you are married.

36. If a pre-nuptial is required it should be discussed before marriage.

Married Financial Considerations

37. In order to make your marriage work you can't have any hidden accounts or purchases.

38. When making your budget use the term 'we' instead of 'I.' This concept helps build your financial wealth as a team. This shows that your marriage is built upon one vision.

39. Allow the spouse with the most financial wisdom to organize and lead the household's budget.

40. If you are already married, make sure you and your spouse discuss finances on a bi-weekly or monthly basis; especially if you have joint accounts.

41. If possible, try to live off of one income and allow the spouse's income to go towards savings, vacations, etc. (This works well if your marriage starts with this principle.)

42. Don't compare yourself to other couples. Everyone's financial goals are not the same.

43. Designate one person who will be responsible for actually doing the task of paying the bills.

44. Be open to share your financial fears with your spouse. This will help you avoid pitfalls.

Chapter Five
The Law of Dining

Eating well is one of the greatest benefits of being on God's earth!

Psalm 104:14-15 states that, *"He causes the grass to grow for the cattle and vegetation for the service of man, that he may bring forth food from the earth. And wine that makes glad the heart of man. Oil to make his face shine. And bread which strengthens man's heart."*

So know it is God's design for you to eat well. But in those scriptures it was never discussed to spend frivolously to enjoy these benefits. In this chapter we will explore ways to eat great and save money at the same time.

Restaurants

1. Always consider water as your beverage of choice.

2. Dine at expensive restaurants during lunch time as opposed to dinner time.

3. Check and see if your area offers a Restaurant Week.

4. This allows you to try great places at affordable prices.

5. Go to restaurants during 'Happy Hour' and only order from the promotion menu.

6. Pay attention to flyers in the mail for local restaurants.

7. When splitting the tab with friends only pay for what you order. This will eliminate overpaying for food you didn't eat.

8. Pay attention to applications like Yelp, Groupon, and LivingSocial. These are a great source guides to the city's excellent eateries and great deals.

9. Be nice to whomever you encounter on the restaurant staff and remain low maintenance. This opens doors for under the table discounts. For example: I was recently dining at a restaurant that ran out of the desert I desperately wanted. After informing the item was sold out, they went the extra mile and allowed me to select another desert of my choice at no cost.

10. Gratuity for a meal should always be between 15% and 20%. If you received exceptional service you have an option to tip greater than 20%.

11. Limit your specialty beverage choices. This increases your total gratuity amount.

12. Be mindful of how you customize your meal. Example: adding extra cheese or substituting an entrée item.

13. Observe restaurant meal specials. Example: 2 for $20 or 3 courses for $30.

14. Pay attention to your receipts. In most cases these offer surveys for free food or discounted meals.

15. When you don't have a heavy appetite stick with salads and appetizers.

16. Order with your wallet not your eyes.

17. When dining out skip the foods that are comfortable. This allows you to expand your meal variety. Plus, by now you should be an expert chef at making comfort food at home.

18. Don't be afraid of leftovers. They always make a great lunch the following day.

19. When eating at a fine restaurant, save on dessert by finding an alternative location. Example: Ice cream shop, or local bakery. For those dating: your date will

be impressed and so will your wallet.

20. Dine at restaurants that offer children's meals or family nights. Example: Golden Corral or Chick-Fil-A.

21. Fill out the customer cards that request your email address. This keeps you in the loop for more promotions.

22. It never hurts to see if the restaurant offers half portion meals.

23. Sunday Brunch is a great time to explore restaurants most of these places offer an affordable brunch or lunch menu.

24. Don't be afraid to explore local restaurants. Their prices are sometimes the same as chain restaurants.

25. When ordering wines and alcoholic drinks try to synchronize your dining experience with their drink special days. Example: if you are craving a mimosa try to order the drink during a brunch experience where they may be only $5 per drink.

26. Dinner for one is always less expensive than dinner for two. Don't be afraid to dine alone. Get dressed up and treat yourself to a nice meal.

Chapter Six
The Law of Shrink My Bills

For many of us BILLS are one of the main reasons we avoid going to our mail boxes, checking our bank accounts or even evading certain people. Understanding paying bills is a necessity to life: we must begin to attack this head on.

Philippians 4:19 states, *"And my God shall supply all your need according to his riches in glory by Christ Jesus."* This means that if we have a need for our bills to decrease, God is the source and able to fulfill our need. In this chapter we will observe ways that you can save money on monthly bills. (. . . and God really helps those who work hard to help themselves!!)

Cable & Television

1. Beware of the equipment fees when it comes to cable/television. See if some of this equipment can be purchased.

2. Set reminders on your phone for the expiration date for your current cable/satellite promotion. Know the current promotion and ask to speak with someone in their retention group to negotiate future fees.

3. Consider cutting the cable cord as a whole. There are many great alternatives like Hulu, Amazon Prime and Netflix. These options allow you to stream television through the Internet.

4. Consider purchasing an HD Television antenna for your local channels. These can be purchased for $20-$30 bucks at Wal-Mart.

Credit Cards

5. Call your credit card company and ask for a lowered interest rate.

6. Consider a balance transfer to a lower interest credit card. Make sure the transfer fees don't outweigh the actual savings.

7. Try to avoid using the credit card as much as possible. Leave it at home and use cash.

Insurance

8. Do comparison-shopping for insurance premiums. Competition keeps companies competitive.

9. Understand what discounts your insurance company offers. Example multiple policies, such as car and home, etc.

10. You can cut your insurance premiums by increasing your deductible.

11. You can cut your insurance premium by opting for liability coverage for any vehicle you have paid off.

Wireless Phones/Home Phone

12. Many employers offer discounts on your wireless bill, phones, and accessories.

13. Consider trading in your old device for a new phone. Apple iPhones typically hold great trade in values.

14. Avoid signing up for two year contracts by purchasing used devices. Be very careful not to purchase stolen devices.

15. Get rid of unnecessary features. Example: insurance, data, or additional lines of unused service.

16. Prepaid phone options have become very affordable. Consider switching from contract to prepay.

This will help you avoid unwanted overages.

17. If you are not one to use the phone regularly consider a VOIP service. Ooma, Magic Jack, and Vonage are great low cost options.

Energy/Gas

18. Check with your energy provider for programs to reduce your energy bills.

19. Utilize your programmable thermostat in your home to reduce heating/cooling cost.

20. Yearly check ups on major appliances like your air conditioner or heater may reduce your yearly energy consumption.

21. Avoid leaving your high-powered technology devices plugged for periods longer than 12 hours of non-use.

Water Bills

22. Research and see if your county offers any water efficient programs. Example: in Durham County, NC they offer a $100 rebate on your water bill for switching to a 1.6 GPF toilet.

23. Decrease the amount of time you spend in the shower.

24. Avoid brushing your teeth with the water running.

25. Only use the dishwasher when you have a full load.

Car Repairs

26. Reduce your car repair expenses by using *quality* aftermarket parts. Before purchasing always check the reviews and ask a trusted mechanic.

27. Call XM/Sirius and request their latest promotional pricing. Paying $14.99 per month for satellite radio is a thing of the past.

28. Always go to your repair shop's website and review their repair specials.

29. If you are looking for a great mechanic always read the reviews and thoughts of others.

30. Use the app RepairPal to help you learn more information about reasonable car repair expenses.

Chapter Seven
The Law of Retail Shopping

In the Bible when kings appeared we always ascribed them with high self-worth because of their position and attire. Peter 2:9 speaks about who we are as believers. It states *"but you are a chosen people, a royal priesthood, a holy nation, God's special possession, that you may declare the praises of Him who called you out of darkness into His wonderful light."*

In other words there is a look and an image of a Christian. This look pertains to your inner and outward appearance. In this chapter we will explore how you make your outer appearance look like that of a king or queen within a limited budget.

Dress for Financial Success

1. Understand the goal of a retailer is to make a profit through markups!!!

2. 50% off is better than Buy One Get One. (BOGO) BOGO promotions force you to purchase two items when you may only need one. If you only need one item consider combining your purchase with a friend.

3. Don't forget the coupons!

4. Sign up for E-Bates. This website gives you cash back for your purchases as well as rebates. This is a great site for online shoppers.

5. Google search for discounts or coupons before you make a purchase.

6. Register your email address with your favorite retailers so that you can receive coupons and special sale invites.

7. 'Family & Friends' sales normally offer 20-30% off items that never go on sale.

8. Remember to shop off-season for staple items. Example: suits, boots, slacks, coats, and sandals.

9. Use Google to help you with comparison-shopping.

10. When there is a certain threshold for free shipping, consider ordering more than one item. Upon arrival return the unwanted item.

11. If your favorite retailer offers a loyalty reward point system that is free, sign up for it.

12. Understand your financial situation. Never go shopping with a friend who just got paid or lacks financial priorities. These friends will often times guilt you into making unnecessary purchases.

13. Don't be afraid of thrift shopping. Many great buys on luxury brand names are purchased in thrift stores. Some thrift stores offer half promotions.

14. Take advantage of price match. Price matching has become easier than ever. With bar code scanning applications the ability to comparison shop on the go is easier than ever.

15. When it's closer to your birthday, try to minimize shopping until your favorite retailers sends birthday coupons.

16. Markdowns take place all of the time in the retail industry. Don't be afraid of price adjustments. Price adjustments happen when the price you paid for something you purchased changes within 7 -14 days. You can go back to the retailer and request the price difference.

17. Sometimes it's all about knowing where to shop. T J Max, Ross, and Marshall's are all great locations to get brand name items for great prices.

18. Outlet stores are a great way to score great deals on normally expensive items. Example: Michael Kors,

Gucci, Off Saks 5th Avenue, Cole Haan, Nike, Polo, J. Crew, Coach.)

19. Don't be afraid to give retailers your phone number. This is mostly used to match your address for mailing coupons.

20. If you are purchasing a display model never be afraid to ask for an additional discount and purchase a warranty. Use this when making technology purchases.

21. Consider purchasing school technology items during No Tax Day weekend.

22. Observe the retailers that allow you to receive coupons on your phone. Couponing can't get any easier than that. Example: Michael's Arts & Crafts.

23. Don't be afraid of the tailor. Purchasing a pair of slacks regular priced at $150 selling for $20 might not be a bad investment if your tailor can make the pants fit you.

24. If you are a person who struggles with wish lists, always request gift cards. Nothing like going shopping having to spend nothing out of pocket.

25. Always look for store sales flyers at the entrance of the store.

26. Always ask the cashier if there are any additional savings at the time of checkout.

27. Social media is a great way to find promotions from

people in your circle of connections.

28. When shopping at Macys outside of your home state, always go the customer service desk to receive your 10% off coupon.

29. When shopping in large shopping centers that require you to pay for parking, find the retailers that will validate your parking.

30. Always read the fine print. Many stores offer great promotions just during certain hours.

31. Pay attention to your mail. Many retailers send out shopping passes on a monthly basis.

32. Sometimes an imperfection can become perfection for you. If you see an imperfection worth fixing, ask for additional savings. Example: replacing a missing button might not be a bad idea.

33. Consider the cost of maintaining those expensive garments. Example: dry cleaning, or even versatility with your current wardrobe.

34. Remember items at the register are intentionally placed there for impulse purchases. However, sometimes these items are to remind you of what you may have forgotten during your shopping experience.

35. Buy what you want, but at a price you can afford. Many times people sacrifice quality trying to stay within a certain price range. Focus on finding what you want and then dong the research for the price you want.

36. Sometimes waiting is the name of the game.

37. Don't be afraid of a good hand me down. Remember you make the clothes look good. Clothing shouldn't make you look good.

38. If you don't see your size on a particular clearance item, see if the retailer will search other locations for that particular item. Take the next step and get them to place the item on hold or ship it to you for free or for a small fee.

39. Identify store managers in stores and get to know them. These are the people who have the power to offer flexibility in promotional sales.

Chapter Eight
The Law of Swap-A-Tunity

A great way to explain the term Swap-A-Tunity would be an example of Judas. Luke 22 speaks about how Judas was given the option to accept 30 pieces of silver or hold on to the consistent God he knew.

The same goes for opportunities within our budget. How many times have we made mistakes spending our money on unnecessary things, only to find we had wasted our money? In this chapter we will explore how small changes in everyday life can have the greatest impact on your financial situation.

Swap -A-Tunity

1. Consider also waiting until a No-Tax Day weekend for all of your big-ticket computer purchases. Most retailers have great promotion pricing and you pay no taxes.

2. Drafting $20 from your paycheck into a Christmas club account bi-weekly will give you $540 when Christmas time arrives.

3. Using the application Gas-Buddy could help you save as much as $.10 per gallon. At 12,000 miles a year that about $1200 per year.

4. Starting to use a minimum of $5 in coupons per week when you grocery shop could lend you $260 savings per year.

5. Start a Keep-The-Change jar. Simply put any change in your pocket at the end of the day in the jar.

6. If you are doing any online shopping consider getting an e-bates account. This will allow you to get rebates for your shopping. Plus this website gives you coupon codes for additional savings.

7. Consider spending more time with your friends who are concerned with their finances. This will help you make healthy budgeting decisions as well.

8. Consider driving your car for two additional years after it is paid off. With a payment of $350 per month, this will give you an additional savings of $8400.

9. Consider not eating out for lunch twice per week. This could save you $1040 in a year's time. Figure is calculated based upon a $10 lunch meal.

10. Consider boycotting the mall for 6 months a year. Based upon monthly spending of $150 on clothing, this could save you $900 per year.

11. College Students: Consider working through college a maximum of 20 hours a week. This will give you $10,400 in income per year. Use these monies towards books, living expenses, and tuition.

12. Consider cutting the budget for the wedding. The savings will make a great down payment when it's time to purchase your home together.

13. Avoiding Starbucks twice a week for a year could save you $442 per year. This is based upon $4.25 per drink.

14. Working part time for 10 hours a week for $10 an hour can increase your income by $5200 a year.

15. Consider a Do-it-Yourself project. The savings here are limitless. Do make sure it is a task you can handle and manage.

16. If you are an hourly employee consider cutting your lunches in half to increase your time worked. 30 minutes per day could equal 2.5 hours per week.

Chapter Nine
The Law of Home Buying & Renting

The home buying process is a bundle of mixed emotions. At times you will feel stressed, happy, depressed, excited, or even anxiousness. All of these feelings are normal. This is a life changing decision and should not be taken lightly. **It is God's design for us to enjoy the benefits of prosperous living.**

Jeremiah 29:5 speaks of establishing wealth. *"Build houses and dwell in them..."* Enjoy this part of your journey to financial success: this is truly a step ordained by God.

Home Sweet Home

1. Purchasing a home is a great step towards building financial wealth.

2. Understand your first home purchase is not your dream home purchase.

3. Be realistic in your must-haves for your new home.

4. Pull your credit report and start disputing any discrepancies. Also, be ready to defend credit accounts.

5. Identify three possible lender programs or get a mortgage broker. A mortgage broker is a one-stop shop person for your entire loan needs. They have relationships with many mortgage lenders and they do the research for you and present you with the options to choose the best option for you.

6. Be prepared for fees and deposits.
    a. Earnest Money: Deposit money is deposited by the buyer under contract terms to be forfeited if the buyer defaults, but credited to the purchase price if the home closes.
    b. Loan Origination Fee: An administrative fee charged to the borrower by the lender for making a mortgage loan. The fee is used to complete paperwork for a mortgage.
    c. Due Diligence: A fee paid by the buyer to investigate a property of interest. This process is where experts inspect the property and examine titles/liens.
    d. Home Inspection: A thorough inspection,

completed by a licensed inspector, is designed to reveal any defect with your property of choice. Please know this is highly recommended whether new construction or existing construction.

7. Don't be afraid to negotiate the price or ask for what you want. The worst answer you can get is a 'No.' But you don't have a chance of 'yes' if you don't ask.

8. Definitely ask the seller to provide a home warranty, if they don't get one, get one for yourself,. These policies typically start at $400 year. A home warranty covers expensive repairs related to owning a home. This also gives you peace of mind while owning your home. Example: If your A/C breaks down or your need a new hot water heater, then your home warranty would cover those repairs.

9. Some insurance companies offer discounts for having a home security system.

10. Consider foreclosure sales; many properties are turnkey ready.

11. Find out how much home you can afford. Your mortgage including principal, interest, taxes, insurance, and re-occurring debts should not be above 36% of your income. If your income fluctuates, base your affordability from your worst year. Example: if you make $3000 per month multiplied by .36, then the most home and debt you can afford per month is $1080. A VA loan is a 41% debt to income ratio.

12. Don't feel the urge to go into debt furnishing your

entire home upon moving in it. Take it a room at a time. There are no laws mandating this. And typically when you do this you grow out of your home very quickly causing you to feel the need for more space.

13. When you are viewing your prospective home look at the potential of the home. If it's not exactly the way you want it, see if these are affordable things you can change. Paint colors, backsplashes, countertops, cabinet handles, flooring, etc.

14. Don't rely on your realtor to do all of the work to find your dream home. The Internet has made it easy to do your home search.

15. If you have been living in an area for over 3 years, you might want to consider purchasing property in that area.

16. There are many different types of mortgages:
  a. Fixed Rate: A fixed rate for a fixed amount of time. These loans are typically 15, 20, or 30 years.
  b. ARM: Adjustable Rate Mortgage: These mortgage rates adjust with the market. Typically a great option for those persons who do not want to stay in a home long term.
  c. Interest Only Loan: In this loan you are only paying the interest for a certain period of time. This is more common for someone who knows his or her income will increase over time due to a lucrative career. This type of mortgage can be extremely dangerous and you could lose your home since you are never putting a penny on the principle, you are not building any equity in your

home.

17. Location, Location, Location: The re-sale value of your home is most of the time based upon school systems, transportation lines, crime rates, and convenience.

18. LTV: Loan to Value: This is a ratio that compares the value of your loan to the value of a property. You may see this worded as banks requiring 90% LTV. This simply means that you must come up with a 10% down payment in order to process a loan.

19. Understand which home improvements provide the greatest increase in the value of your home. Example: laminate floors in a 1.5 million dollar home will not get you your intended return on investment. Buyers in this price range are expecting hardwood flooring or high-end tile, especially if you live West of the Mississippi.

20. Don't be afraid to purchase a second property. This is excellent rental income.

21. Home ownership comes with many perks and benefits. Example: interest and property taxes are tax deductible.

22. When purchasing new construction don't feel pressured to get your home fully optioned out. Example: rolling a stainless steel appliance into the purchase price of your home only means you are paying on the appliance for the life of the mortgage.

23. Do your research for down payment assistance.

There are many programs for low-income families and first time homebuyers.

24. Consider getting your homeowner's insurance through your car insurance provider. Many of these companies offer discounts for bundling.

25. You will have time to investigate your potential property during the 'due diligence' period. This allows you to do inspections and negotiate any repairs that must be made by the seller.

26. Avoid opening new credit accounts until after you have closed on your home. This is a red flag for mortgage lenders.

27. Home equity is simply the difference between your loan balance and the value of your home. This is very important because sometimes you can avoid paying Private Mortgage insurance (PMI) if you have enough equity in your home. (The money you put down on your home immediately creates this equity. Putting down at least 10% of the price of the home is good, but 20% down is the requirement for not needing PMI.

28. When looking at homes, remember the home that's waiting for you will feel like home upon entering. You will immediately see your furniture, family, and friends in it.

29. Pray through the entire home buying process. Favor exists in home buying!!!

30. Observe housing trends. This will help you get the

most equity in your home. If you notice a trend of more people moving into town, then you might want to move into town or close access to it.

31. You have the right to appeal property taxes if you feel they are too high. Check with your local county government on how to do this. This is an easy way to decrease your tax expenses.

32. Review your mortgage to make sure there are no prepayment penalties involved. A prepayment penalty is a fee charged for paying off a loan early.

33. Most people purchase a home larger than their previous apartment. Don't forget to factor into your monthly budget the percentage increase in your utility bills.

34. If at all possible, stay away from your retirement savings accounts for your down payment.

35. Always ask the seller to pay your closing cost or give you a credit toward it.

36. The best way to know if you are in the right neighborhood is to drive by the area at night or during the weekend.

37. Your realtor won't be able to talk about crime or familial status of a neighborhood. It is up to you to do this research. So talk to the neighbors to find out about the history of the home, problems, deaths, and any unusual issues. This can save a lot of heartache later. Other information can be found publicly online.

38. Try to move into your new home around the timeframe of your tax refund or company bonus.

39. Don't purchase a home worth the full value of your pre-approval. Remember you want to live after purchasing your home.

40. Consider living with family/friends for a few months or a year to save up a large down payment for your home.

41. Make it your goal to have your home paid for before entering into your retirement.

42. Consider setting up your mortgage for bi-weekly payments. This will decrease your mortgage term by 5 years or more. Or consider paying one additional payment per year towards the principle of your home. This will decrease your mortgage by 4 years or more.

43. Don't change jobs in the midst of the mortgage process. The longer you have been with you're your employer, the more stable you will seem to your lender and you will decrease the chances of default.

Chapter Ten
25 Commandments to Do with Money Saved

Saving money is great, but the end result of how the saved money is used is more important. We should use this concept to save for the future. There is a parable in the Bible in Matthew 25:14-28 about three men who were given bags of gold. One was given 5 bags of gold, another 2 bags of gold, and the other 1 bag of gold. This story is symbolic of how believers should manage their money.

To the man who was given 5 talents of gold, put his monies to work and gained 5 more talents. The man who was given two bags of gold gained two bags of gold. Now to the man who was given one bag of gold hid his bag in the ground. Now when it came time to speak with the master about their investments, the master replied to those who gained, *"Well done, good and faithful servant; you were faithful over a few things, I will put you ruler over many things. Enter into the joy of your Lord."*

Now to the man who hid his talents, the master was disappointed and stated that he should have at least placed the gold with a bank to gain interest.

Based upon this parable we can see that favor is found in investing your savings. Dishonor is found in just hiding it. Based upon our finances, many of us feel as though we only have one bag of gold and it's best to spend everything we have to live.

But imagine if we took on the mindset of the first two men in this chapter and invested our bags of gold. Then we would have double the bags of gold. In this chapter we will explore 25 things to do with your savings.

Basic Financial Rules

1. Start paying your tithes and offering.

2. Open a savings account.

3. Start an emergency fund.

4. Increase contributions into your 401k Savings.

5. Pay off debt: It only makes sense to pay down any debt that carries interest.

6. Save up for a down payment on a car.

7. Save up for a down payment on a home.

8. Save up to purchase a much-wanted item as opposed to placing it on a credit card.

9. Open a Christmas club savings account.

10. Pay for 6-12 months of car insurance in advance. **Some insurance companies charge monthly fees for processing payments. This decreases those fees. As well this is one less pre-paid fixed expense**

11. Save up for a vacation.

12. Save up for a wedding.

13. Start a business.

14. Go back to college.

15. Purchase life/burial insurance.

16. Open an investment account and purchase stocks.

17. Pay off a car loan.

18. Make an extra mortgage payment.

19. Pick up a trade career that allows you to work at your own pace. Example: real estate, nails, hair, massage, certified nursing assistant or nursing.

20. Put savings away for your children's education.

21. Give to the needy or charity.

22. Go shopping for a professional wardrobe, but give used items to a consignment shop.

23. Purchase new equipment for your business.

24. Obtain an affordable gym membership.

25. Complete a home improvement project that increases home value.

Chapter Eleven
The Law of Travel

One of the most rewarding things about working hard is being able to play hard. Many times we tend to get this confused with a moment to splurge. This is actually the time to make wise expensive travel decisions.

Through making these decisions you will be able to accomplish even more on your next vacation. Life is filled with many destinations, hopefully through these tips you will be able to explore and still have money in your pockets.

Traveling allows you to behold the beauty of God's Earth.

Explore Your World

1. Always plan ahead.

2. Flights are generally cheaper on Tuesday and Wednesday.

3. When traveling last minute consider an application called Hotel Tonight. This application allows you to purchase hotels last minute at great prices.

4. Utilize email alerts. www.AirFareWatchDog is a website that allows you to watch flight fares and sends them to you daily via email.

5. Traveling off-season is always affordable. When you want to experience the summer weather then consider traveling in the month of September or October.

6. Purchase a membership to American Automobile Association (AAA). This gives you access to discounts for all of your travel needs.

7. Ask your friends for recommendations for cities.

8. Utilize search engine websites such as, Orbitz, Expedia, Priceline, etc.

9. Traveling with friends can reduce the cost of lodging if you are sharing a room.

10. Sometimes it might be cheaper to book a suite as opposed to purchasing two separate rooms.

11. Buddy Passes and Friends & Family discounts are a great way to save major money. But you must have a flexible travel schedule.

12. Become loyal to a hotel chain that rewards your loyalty. Example: Hyatt Rewards, Marriott Rewards, etc. These rewards can equate to discounts or even free hotel stays.

13. Don't be afraid of timeshare tours for low cost vacation get-a-ways.

14. When cruising, remember most islands experience spring and summer weather all year long. So consider a cruise/all-inclusive vacation in December, which is very inexpensive and affordable.

15. When traveling, limit your meal consumption to one GREAT meal per day.

16. Traveling becomes cheaper when you can crash at a friend or family member's pad.

17. Don't waste your money traveling first class. The goal is to arrive to the destination.

18. When renting a car, avoid hotels that charge for valet and overnight parking.

19. Avoid hotels that don't have a cancellation policy. These are sometimes traps.

20. When flying, check the rates to fly in on Monday morning. Most of the time flights are much cheaper.

21. Before booking a flight/hotel online call the actual location. Sometimes there are better deals just for calling.

22. When booking flights consider airlines within an 80-mile radius. You will be amazed at the possible savings.

23. Check the prices after your purchase to see if they have decreased. If so then, contact the company for a credit, refund, or discount on a future flight/stay.

24. If you are not happy with a service with a hotel, airline, or rental car company, let management know. If the outcome isn't satisfactory, then write or contact corporate. Always play the loyalty card or express your desire to become a loyal customer.

25. Be aware of fees associated with air travel. Example: Southwest is one of the few airlines that does not charge passengers for checked baggage.

26. When traveling to larger cities with public transportation opt out of getting a rental car and use public transportation and taxis.

27. Ask your friends about the main attractions and sites you should visit while on your vacation. This will help you avoid wasting money and time.

28. Consider your vacation goal. For example, if it is to rest, then the views from your hotel room will be most important. If it is just to have a bed to sleep in, then consider a less expensive hotel with an okay view.

29. Sometimes organizations, clubs, banks, or retailers sell discounted theme park tickets. Example: the North Carolina State Employees Credit Union offers discounts on theme park tickets.

30. Don't be afraid to mix business travel and personal travel. If your company will allow, add some vacation time to the trip and enjoy.

31. If you are looking for affordable Caribbean travel then visit http://www.cheapcaribbean.com

32. If you are an AAA member then renting cars with Hertz comes with great perks. Example: AAA does not charge you for additional drivers as long as the additional driver has a AAA membership.

Chapter Twelve
The Law of Retirement

As believers, God makes eternal life possible. And for many of us, he has promised extended life on earth. With more and more people living longer it is very important that we prepare for retirement. And understanding that social security isn't enough to sustain you in your golden years, saving towards your retirement is a necessity. Remember on the Sabbath day even Jesus rested.

You can't afford not to save for retirement. Make it as critical a necessity as eating.

Living Well Later in Life

1. 401k accounts are made up of stocks, bonds, mutual funds, and money market investments.

2. Minimum savings for retirement is 10%-15% of your income, which includes whatever you company matches.

3. When reviewing your savings in your retirement account, make sure that you account for any medical conditions you may have upon retiring. Medical needs can be costly in retirement.

4. Find out how long you must work in your company before you are vested. This is the time period when company match money becomes yours. The sooner the better.

5. ROTH is funded through after tax monies. Once the participant reaches age 59.5 the gains are free from taxes.

6. Do a check-up with your retirement account every 6-8 months. Investment strategies are like fashion trends, they CHANGE, so what worked 2 years ago may not work today.

7. If you are unfamiliar with investments,choose a target date fund. These fund dates are based upon the year you want to retire and your age now.

8. Increase you contributions as often as possible. Most

companies offer an annual increase program.

9. Beware of the "10% early withdrawal penalty." This penalty applies when you withdraw funds from your account before age 59 1/2.

10. Before withdrawing money from a retirement account consider adjusting your budget or getting a part time job.

11. If you withdraw money from a retirement account those monies are considered taxable income and can change your tax bracket.

12. If you have left your employer, consult with your investment firm to see if it's best to leave the money in the plan or roll it over to an IRA (individual retirement account.)

13. A retirement account does not negate the need for bank savings accounts. Make sure you have a balance between the two. Retirement accounts are harder to access for emergency needs.

14. If you must touch your retirement account because of an emergency situation, please consider a loan instead. The loan option allows you to avoid penalties. Both of these transactions decrease the ability of your account to grow.

15. The maximum you can put away in any 401k, 403b and most 457 accounts is $18,000 yearly. Starting the year in which you turn age 50, the IRS will allow you to do catch-up contributions. This is an additional $6,000

yearly. This is based upon the guidelines from the IRS for 2015.

16. If you are self-employed, then consider a self-employed 401K account, or an IRA account. These accounts are commonly found at Fidelity Investments.

17. Be aware: In their 20's, people say I have time. In their 30's, they say: I'll start saving, but only the minimum. When they're in their 40's, people realize they haven't saved enough. Once they hit their 50's, they start saving and realize too late that they may not reach their retirement savings goal. These accounts don't grow overnight. Don't be discouraged by a one-day loss. Think long term, because growth of retirement accounts is based upon contributions plus growth of monies being invested.

18. Place a larger part of your bonus monies into your retirement account.

19. If you are in need of tax deductions to lower your taxable income then consider contributing into your account on a pre-tax basis.

20. As you get closer to your retirement age consider placing the majority of your money in a stable fund.

21. Never place all of your money in one investment. The key to successful return on your investment is *diversification*.

22. If your finances are tight it is better to put away *something* rather than *nothing*. This is extremely important

if your company has a match program. Example: Deferring 1% of your salary is better than 0%. Especially if your company has a funds matching program.

23. Consult with an investment advisor to come up with an investment strategy to meet your retirement needs.

24. Observe this list: do not use your retirement account for any of the five things listed below. None of these items will ever make money for you.
   a. Paying off credit cards
   b. Paying living expenses
   c. Buying Cars
   d. Shopping
   e. Weddings/Vacations

25. Once you reach retirement, your goal is to have little or no debt.

26. Make sure you assign/review your beneficiaries.

About the Author

Milburn T. Simmons (M. T. Simmons) has found a passion for helping everyone excel with his or her finances. He has observed that many people lack the proper foundation for financial success. Simmons believes it is his responsibility to help these people reach their full potential. He has been able to do this through motivational tips on social media, financial consultations, workshops, and seminars.

Prior to starting Broke2Rich, M. T. Simmons used experiences from his life and career as a qualification to empower others regarding their finances. Since leaving his hometown, Goldsboro, NC to complete his baccalaureate degree from North Carolina Central University, his career experiences have included: banking, wireless technology, retirement services, sales, management, customer service and budget analysis.

Currently M.T. Simmons resides in the Raleigh/Durham, North Carolina area. He is a realtor, author, blogger, motivational speaker, and community volunteer.

Contact M.T. Simmons to learn more about his speaking schedule, at: www.broke2rich.net